A Cotman-Color Book with
text by **E. A. Ellis**

Wild Flowers of the Waterways and Marshes

Jarrold Colour Publications, Norwich

1

1. MARSH MARIGOLD (*Caltha palustris*). These are the 'Mary-buds' which paint the meadows with delight in early spring. They are also known as 'King-cups'. Their deep gold chalices shine in great clusters, nestling in marshes and along the shores of waterways all over Britain. They are very plentiful in stubbles left by reed-cutters round the Norfolk Broads. In these giant buttercups yellow sepals take the place of petals. The flowers attract many insects, including butterflies which have just come out of hibernation.

The plant life of our waterways is richly varied and its beauty lies very much in the pattern of its zonation, beginning with the lilies and translucent pondweeds of open water and developing in natural succession by way of bulrush swamps and reed-beds, the rich and colourful vegetation of fens and water-meadows to an ultimate realm of willows and dark alders. In deep, clear waters plants with wholly submerged leaves predominate while in shallows nearer inshore more species have floating leaves. These pioneers produce a litter of peaty remains when their leaves and stems decay in winter, gradually raising the level of mud at the bottom. There comes a time when pools are shallow enough to permit invasion by tall plants such as bulrushes, reed-maces and reeds. These in turn thicken and consolidate the mud, preparing the way for a greater range of marsh plants which first occupy the higher niches on reed and sedge tufts and later take over more and more of the ground as the level goes on rising. Many of the marshes which have evolved naturally in this way become modified by Man cutting reeds for thatch, mowing fens for hay and introducing livestock where conditions are favourable. Wild animals such as voles and rabbits also play a selective part in the later stages of marsh development, tending to encourage an increase in dwarf plants as the canopy of taller, coarser vegetation is reduced. Extensive peat-cutting has been carried out in many of our older marshes over the centuries, resulting in the creation of new pools, including some very extensive ones such as exist today as the Norfolk Broads. In these instances human interference has put the clock back to the beginning and the whole process of change must make a fresh start. At the opposite extreme great tracts of fenland have been drained to provide rich soil for agriculture, and in such areas the aquatic and marsh vegetation is now confined to the ditches. Where the build-up of marshes is not deflected artificially, accumulating residues of sedges and herbs eventually pile up and reach a level at which there is no flushing by mineral residues in mud between occasional winter floods, so that the highest peat is apt to be colonised by spongy bog mosses, sundews and other plants characteristic of acid peat soils. Sooner or later any opening in the ground canopy gives tree seedlings a chance to establish themselves. Marshes left to themselves long enough become completely overgrown by scrub consisting of sallow bushes or alders, usually mixed with berry-bearing species such as the two buckthorns, guelder rose and spindle. Finally when the land surface stands high enough, marsh gives place to forests of oak, ash and hazel or birch and pine.

Many of our marsh and water plants are of the same species as those which flourished in Britain half a million years ago; but they have not occupied this country continuously, owing to the intervention of a series of ice-ages. The last of the ice-sheets retreated sufficiently for vegetation to reappear about fifteen thousand years ago. There were extensive lakes and swamps filling every hollow of the land when the ice-caps melted. At first the wild flowers were similar to those now typical of the arctic tundras, but as the climate became less cold more and more species from temperate regions spread northwards to replace them. For a while this country experienced a hotter and drier climate than that prevailing now; this was followed by a long period of warm, wet years and a further very dry epoch before the weather pattern reached its present phase a little over two thousand years ago. Up to 6000 B.C. East Anglia was joined to the mainland of Europe by a vast lowland region of dunes, forests, marshes, lakes and rivers forming a convenient bridge for invasion by Continental plants. Shortly afterwards the whole area became submerged beneath the rising waters of the North Sea. At the same time, forests occupying valleys towards what is now our east coast were drowned by the local rivers and this inundation was followed by a great upsurge of freshwater life in the regions affected. While climatic history has played an important part in determining the present pattern of our waterways and their associated flora, many other factors are also involved. Some plants cannot tolerate 'hard' alkaline waters and are therefore absent where rivers and springs stem from limestone or chalk and where surface waters drain from chalky boulder clay. At the other extreme there are species restricted to places where there is an abundance of lime. Water plants differ in their abilities to cope with such things as scouring by fast currents in streams, turbulence which keeps water cloudy with mud in suspension, various forms of chemical pollution, temporary flooding by salt water and so on. In places which are wet for only part of the year, such as many of our shallower ponds, one finds water and mud plants specially adapted to this way of life; but there are many species which must be immersed in water perpetually to survive. Even a slight permanent lowering of the water-table in a peat-marsh has a very marked effect on certain species and much less on others.

Aquatic and waterside plants in many cases have floating seeds which are dispersed by drifting in floods. Very small seeds and others equipped with burry hooks may be carried long distances by migrating ducks and wading birds. In other cases the seeds have silken parachutes and are transported by winds in dry weather. Many waterweeds produce special 'resting buds' which break away from the parents and lie in the mud during the winter, and when spring comes, they rise to the surface, drifting for a time before settling down again in new positions. Some of the more aggressive perennials dominating the scene increase their hold by means of subterranean runners; thus an extensive reed-bed often develops from just one seedling. Although there is an appearance of serenity in wide green valleys and quiet pools, the wetlands are for ever in a state of flux, with constant battles for ascendancy in progress between competing plants, so that the scene changes year by year. It is not so very long since the first colonists arrived in the wake of the glaciers; other species have followed in rich procession down the years and we still find newcomers like the Canadian water-thyme, monkey-flower and the orange and Himalayan balsams joining the throng with spectacular success in our time. The spectrum of beauty in a marsh-scape must always awaken a sense of adventure in those who behold it in depth as well as breadth.

The rhythm of the seasons is apparent in the quick surge of growth in spring, the rich blossoming of summer and the flaring gold of reeds in autumn. Waterweeds harbour a teeming life of insects and molluscs. Dragonflies, metallic reed-beetles, special butterflies, moths, bugs and spiders throng meadows and jungles in rich procession from the time marsh marigolds and pussy willow catkins appear until the reed plumes are fluffing at the approach of winter. Wildfowl haunt the open waters and nest secretly in the neighbouring swamps which also harbour countless little chattering warblers in summer. Otter, water-vole and water-shrew frolic there and the diminutive harvest-mouse weaves nests about the reed stalks. At every level the vegetation provides shelter and sustenance for animal life in great variety. One has to move rather slowly and carefully in swampy places, so there is always time to stand and stare. Botanising brings many incidental delights which increase with a growing understanding of plant-and-animal relationships. One soon discovers how sharply the patterns of communities reflect even small changes in the environment and how easily the balance is disturbed by human interference. The wildflowers of waterways and marshes are a very significant and precious part of our wildlife inheritance.

2. LADY'S-SMOCK (*Cardamine pratensis*). Also called the 'Cuckoo-flower' because it comes into bloom just as cuckoos are returning in spring. It grows most profusely in meadows lightly grazed or mown for hay in summer. The cress-like leaves can be eaten in salads and they are a favourite food of the caterpillars of Orange-tip butterflies. New plants often arise as sprouts from leaflets broken off and dispersed by winter floods. The flowers vary from white to a rich mauve colour and 'double' forms are not uncommon.

3. COMMON OSIER (*Salix viminalis*). The most popular of osiers used in basket-making, it has very long, pliant stems, usually obtained by pollarding the stocks close to the ground in the osier-beds. As in all willows, the male and female catkins are produced on separate trees early in spring; they yield abundant nectar which attracts bees and butterflies. Later, the female trees release quantities of fluffy seeds which colonise bare mud, such as that provided by river dredgings.

4. ALDER (*Alnus glutinosa*). This tree flourishes on wet, peaty ground and has reddish bacterial nodules on its roots to assist in the assimilation of nitrates in this somewhat acid watery habitat. The crimson and gold lamb's-tail catkins appear before the leaves in March and April and the female flowers eventually mature to resemble miniature fir-cones packed with rust-coloured seeds. The seeds are scattered when birds attack the cones in winter; they float on the water and are spread widely by winter floods. Alder wood is used for making casks and drain-pipes.

5. TUFTED SEDGE (*Carex elata*). This sedge with characteristically blue-green leaves flowers alongside fen ditches in spring. It forms compact tufts which consolidate the shores, preventing erosion; but it does not put forth underwater shoots and invade open water like some other mud-plants. It is more tolerant of shade than most other sedges and continues to thrive long after marshes have become overgrown by alders and willows. It is the chief food plant of a slender bug matching the colour of its leaves.

6. COLUMBINE (*Aquilegia vulgaris*). The natural haunts of wild columbines in England include sedge beds partly shaded by alders in some of our river valleys; but the flowers can also be found on limestone slopes and in damp oak glades occasionally. The old-fashioned forms grown in cottage gardens are largely derived from the wild form while the many-coloured modern varieties consist of hybrids between these and some North American species. The wing-like sepals and curved spurs resemble miniature doves in appearance.

7. SNAKE'S-HEAD (*Fritillaria meleagris*). These purple or sometimes milk-white chequered lilies used to be plentiful on many water-meadows in the south and east of England. Now they survive in only a few of their old haunts and people make pilgrimages to enjoy the beauty of their massed blossoms annually at the end of April. They persist most successfully where the meadows are mown or grazed every summer after the plants have seeded. This treatment controls tall vegetation which would otherwise overgrow them and rob the seedlings of the sunlight required for early growth.

8. BOG-BEAN (*Menyanthes trifoliata*). A near relative of the gentians, this common plant of bog pools bears its pink and white star-flowers in May and June in the lowlands, but later at higher altitudes. The petals are faced and fringed with little white threads which glitter like spun glass, giving the blossoms the beauty of frost crystals. This species has a wide range over the northern hemisphere. Prehistoric peoples made flour and bread from its pounded roots and the leaves have been used like hops in brewing.

9. RAGGED ROBIN (*Lychnis flos-cuculi*). This bright magenta marsh campion with finely divided petals flowers most freely where trees and other tall plants have been removed in the previous season. It needs good illumination and plenty of space to grow to perfection. The blossoms appear from May to July and attract many insects, including bumble bees. They are great favourites with swallowtail butterflies round the Norfolk Broads. Their delicate clove scent draws moths at night.

10. SMALL-FLOWERED YELLOWCRESS (*Barbarea stricta*). Although this waterside plant is widely distributed in Europe it is comparatively rare in this country, where it is reckoned to be an invader of fairly recent origin. It appears chiefly along the lower reaches of rivers where the water tends to rise and fall with the tides. Seedlings become established only at the highest tide level and where they get plenty of sunlight. The slender spikes of pale yellow flowers rise from basal rosettes of leaves in June and produce stiffly erect pods.

11. WATER CROWFOOT (*Ranunculus heterophyllus*). This is one of several small white buttercups which grow in ponds, ditches and streams. The massed blossoms sometimes look like snowdrifts on some of our shallower village ponds. All the submerged leaves are thready and fennel-like, but those reaching the surface are broadly kidney-shaped with marginal indentations and display a glossy upper surface. These plants are very adaptable and able to survive in a dwarfed state when ponds dry up.

12

13

12. YELLOW FLAG (*Iris pseudacorus*). This wild iris grows in marshes and by pools and streams throughout Britain. It flowers most freely where the plants are exposed to plenty of light; in shady places only the sword-like leaves develop year after year. Fleshy, sausage-shaped rhizomes spread just beneath the surface of swampy ground, forming rafts which provide a safe support for walkers who venture into its quaggy haunts. In autumn clusters of green pods split open and shed quantities of reddish-brown floatable seeds.

13. WATER VIOLET (*Hottonia palustris*). An aquatic member of the primrose family, known anciently as the 'Water Gillofer', this elegant plant flourishes in pools and ditches in many parts of England, being commonest in the eastern counties. The yellow-green leaves are finely divided and comb-like, remaining submerged. The lilac-coloured blossoms with deep yellow throats emerge in whorled spikes above the water in May and June. The roots are black with white tips which glisten like crystals.

14. EARLY MARSH ORCHID (*Dactylorhiza incarnata*). This species begins flowering in May, a month before the Common Marsh Orchid comes into bloom. It can be found in fens and bogs throughout Britain. The flowers are typically flesh pink, but may be brick red, rosy, bright purple, sulphur-yellow or white. They are crowded in cylindrical spikes and have diamond-shaped, 'pinched' lips, thick spurs and curved, wing-like outer petals. The leaves are rather narrow, yellow-green, stiffly sword-shaped and hooded at the tips.

15. GUELDER ROSE (*Viburnum opulus*). Known anciently as 'Gattridge' or 'Marrish Elder', this deciduous shrub of fens and marshes grows most plentifully where lime is present. The milk-white flowers appear in June, the outermost being sterile, with large, showy petals, while those in the centre are fertile and less conspicuous. They fill the air with a heavy perfume and attract moths by night. Towards the end of summer the leaves turn scarlet and crimson while clusters of brilliant red berries attract fieldfares, waxwings and other winter bird visitors.

16. MEADOWSWEET (*Filipendula ulmaria*).

The creamy, fragrant flowers of this plant form vast swards on many water-meadows in July, tending to dominate other vegetation. In some places the plants are mown for hay while in their prime; they then sprout afresh and yield a fresh crop of blossoms in the autumn. The foliage has a gently astringent quality and is an excellent and palatable food for livestock. A pleasant drink can be made from the flowers and it is said to relieve stomach-ache.

17. TUFTED VETCH (*Vicia cracca*).

This scrambling climber is common in rough, bushy grassland and by roadsides; it is often luxuriant on our drier fens. Growing to a height of six feet, it produces crest-like heads of small, violet-blue flowers in long succession from June onwards through the summer. In dry situations the foliage appears silvery from the presence of short, silky hairs which develop on the leaves to conserve moisture. English country names for this plant include 'Blue Tar-fitch', 'Huggaback', and 'Mousepea'.

18. COMMON MARSH ORCHID (*Dactylorhiza praetermissa*).

This grows plentifully in many water-meadows, fens and wet, peaty places mainly in the southern half of England. The flowers are mostly pinkish purple, but may be very pale pink or white. Typically the leaves are green and unspotted, but one finds many confusing forms which arise from hybridisation with Spotted Orchids. The flower spikes are usually more conical than those of the Early Marsh Orchid and the individual blossoms are larger, with broad lower petals.

19. MARSH CINQUEFOIL (*Potentilla palustris*). A creeping perennial often associated with bog-bean and rushes in the wetter, more open parts of bogs and fens. The leaves have five finger-like silvery-green leaflets and the flowers are peculiar in having dull, wine-red sepals spread in five-pointed stars which are more conspicuous than the much smaller petals. The fruits are purple and superficially resemble strawberries except that they lack the succulent flesh. This species ranges from temperate to arctic regions.

20. GREATER SPEARWORT (*Ranunculus lingua*). This very tall buttercup with long spear-shaped leaves grows in reed-swamps and peaty pools. It has a wide distribution in Britain but tends to be narrowly localised and rare in most counties. It grows to perfection when rooted in water; plants associated with sedges in fens are less vigorous and are commonly damaged by slugs and insects. In some places yellow cluster-cups of a rust-fungus appear on the leaves in June and their spores infect reeds during the rest of the summer.

21. YELLOW WATER-LILY (*Nuphar lutea*). Our commonest water-lily, this species tolerates fairly swift currents in our rivers and may even survive where mud in suspension clouds the water for most of the time. Once the massive rootstocks are established it maintains a tena-cious hold and is difficult to control by weed-cutting where it obstructs navigation. When not in bloom the leaves can be recognised by the veins running parallel with the midrib while the stalks are triangular in section. The poppy-like fruits persist above the water and eventually release jelly-bags of black seeds.

22. WHITE WATER-LILY (*Nymphaea alba*). In the Middle Ages the flowers were known as 'Water Roses'. They are to be found chiefly in still pools and lakes rather than in running water. The giant leaves are green and glossy above and purple underneath and may have stalks up to ten feet long rising from the depths. The 'brandy-bottle' fruits bob at the surface of the water for a while and then become submerged, finally liberating countless small pink seeds.

23. MARSH PEA (*Lathyrus palustris*). This amethyst-blue vetchling is confined to reedy fens and in Britain its main haunts are in East Anglia. It avoids acid peat and is therefore absent from true bogs. Fen soils contain traces of lime which appear essential for the survival of this species. The habitat must also be constantly moist and this plant has been exterminated in many places by over-draining. A delicate relative of the everlasting-peas grown in gardens, it entwines the stems of reeds.

24. WATER BISTORT (*Polygonum amphibium*). This amphibious species grows very adaptably in waters of varying depth. In ponds and lakes the leaves are smooth and more or less heart-shaped; they have very long stalks and float on the surface. The bright pink, cylindrical flower-heads stand out of the water in late summer. A form found growing away from the water looks very different. It has silky, willow-like leaves which are held erect and lack stalks. This land form seldom flowers profusely.

25. SWEET FLAG (*Acorus calamus*). A member of the arum family, with yellow-green, curiously rippled sword-shaped leaves, this plant was introduced to our ponds and rivers in the sixteenth century and has since become widely naturalised except in the north. It is believed to have come originally from southern Asia. At one time the leaves were strewn with rushes on the floors of churches and houses to sweeten the atmosphere. They have a powerful vanilla-like scent when crushed.

26. ARROW-HEAD (*Sagittaria sagittifolia*). A common plant of slow-flowing lowland rivers, it sends up a series of three types of leaves from the bottom. Some are like long, light green grass-blades streaming translucently in the currents; some are oval and lie flat on the surface of the water while others are boldly arrow-shaped and emergent, like the flower-spikes which appear with them from July onwards. The flowers are unisexual, with the male whorls uppermost.

25

26

27. PURPLE LOOSESTRIFE (*Lythrum salicaria*). This tall and showy species grows along the banks of our lowland rivers and canals and is quick to colonise bare patches of peat in marshes. Its seeds will only germinate in direct sunlight and this is why the plant is largely restricted to open situations. The flowers are of three distinct forms, each with stamens and pistils of differing length-ratios. This facilitates cross-pollination by insects.

28. BOG PIMPERNEL (*Anagallis tenella*). A prostrate creeping plant of peaty soil, often abundant round the edges of pools in bogs and spreading over moss in closely grazed wet turf. Where the habitat is exposed to plenty of light, great numbers of the pink blossoms carpet the ground in summer. This species is very sensitive to drought and soon disappears when fens and bogs are drained. Conversely, it is quick to increase where the drainage of low meadows is obstructed.

29. MARSH WOUNDWORT (*Stachys palustris*). Unlike the common Hedge Woundwort, which is noted for its powerful foetid odour, this species has scentless leaves. It develops long underground shoots which bear tubers resembling miniature Chinese Artichokes which are the product of a closely related plant, *Stachys sieboldii*. The light purple flowers appear from July onwards in water-meadows, fens and along the banks of lowland streams and ditches.

30. YELLOW LOOSESTRIFE (*Lysimachia vulgaris*). A late summer flower of riversides and fens, it ranges over most of Britain, but becomes rarer northwards. A member of the primrose family, this herbaceous perennial yellow pimpernel is quite unrelated to the Purple Loosestrife. The flowers are not much visited by insects, but one kind of bee is specially partial to them. The willowy leaves are the only food of a rare weevil. An excellent yellow dye can be extracted from the flowers.

31. MARSH HELLEBORINE (*Epipactis palustris*). This orchid with rather broad leaves is often found growing in large patches in rushy fens, wet heaths and the peaty hollows of old sand dunes. Colonies develop from single plants which spread by means of underground runners. The leaves are cupped at the base to collect dew at night and this helps the plants to survive in a drought. The flowers have spreading platforms on which bees and burnet-moths can alight conveniently.

32. COMMON BLADDER-WORT (*Utricularia vulgaris*).

This rootless, feathery-leaved water plant lives submerged in peaty pools and ditches. Only the butter-yellow 'snap-dragon' flowers appear above the surface, in late summer and autumn. The forked leaf-lets have little bladders which serve as traps for catching small crustaceans and in-sects. Inward-pointing hairs in their mouths allow the prey to creep in, but prevent escape. The plants 'digest' and absorb protein from the bodies of their victims.

33. HEMP AGRIMONY (*Eupatorium cannabinum*). A tall perennial common in a variety of damp habitats where grazing animals are absent. It often grows in large patches, like the stinging nettle, with new shoots springing from below year after year. The large grey-green leaves bear some resemblance to those of hemp. The flattish heads of blossom are usually dusky pink and sometimes white, maturing from July onwards. They are as attractive to butterflies as the purple buddleias of our gardens.

34. MARSH SOWTHISTLE (*Sonchus palustris*). Towering to a height of eight feet, this perennial sowthistle with very pale yellow flowers and arrow-shaped leaves is a rare British plant. It grows on clayey river banks, mainly along the Lower Thames and in the eastern parts of Norfolk and Suffolk. It became almost extinct at the end of the nineteenth century but has since colonised many miles of banks where river dredgings have been deposited, especially behind estuaries. The flowers appear in July and August.

35. WATER MINT (*Mentha aquatica*). The peppermint scent often noticed when one is walking through wet meadows comes from this plant. The aroma varies, sometimes resembling that of eau de cologne or lemon. The peppermint used for flavouring arose in the first instance as a hybrid between this species and the common green spearmint used in the preparation of mint sauce. Tea made from leaves of wild water mint is a gipsy beverage. The flowers come very late in summer and are favourites with bees and butterflies.

36. HIMALAYAN BALSAM (*Impatiens glandulifera*). Also known nowadays as 'Policeman's Helmet', this showy garden plant has escaped and invaded river valleys in Britain on a large scale in recent years. In many places it now covers water-meadows to the exclusion of most of the native wild flowers, growing very tall, with fleshy stems and broad leaves overshading other species. The purple and white flowers are attractive to bees and butterflies and the black seeds are scattered explosively as in other balsams. The seeds float on water.

37. ORANGE BALSAM (*Impatiens capensis*). A native of North America, where it is known as the 'Jewel-weed', this plant was introduced into England in the nineteenth century and has since colonised many of our riversides and marshes. An annual, its seedlings develop rapidly in May and June, producing tall plants with startling orange flowers topping them from July until frosts blacken them in autumn. Bees and wasps visiting the flowers become coated with white pollen. Seeds are catapulted from the green 'spring-loaded' capsules.

38. MARSH FLEABANE (*Pulicaria dysenterica*). This plant matures late in the summer on clayey meadows where most of the vegetation is kept short by grazing animals. The button-headed flowers, at first golden, become a deep ochre colour with age and are succeeded by brown, shortly fluffy seeds. The leaves are cottony underneath and have a strong odour midway between that of cats and chrysanthemums; this discourages cattle from browsing on them. A smouldering bunch of fleabane is said to asphyxiate fleas and other noxious domestic insects.

39. SAW-WORT (*Serratula tinctoria*). A close relative of thistle and knapweeds, this is essentially a plant of damp ground where lime is available and it is commonest in limestone country. The leaves are stiff, sharply toothed and lobed towards the base, but have no true prickles· The flower-heads have a neat, tight-waisted appearance, with smooth scaly bracts holding crowns of plumy purple florets.

40. REED (*Phragmites communis*). Our tallest native grass, sometimes reaching a height of eleven feet, it grows most vigorously in swamps which receive silt and nitrogenous nutrients regularly in seasons of flood or from fertile waters. Its rhizomes spread through the mud, establishing vast reed-beds round the margins of lowland lakes such as the Norfolk Broads. The leafy canes are topped with purplish-brown plumes in August. The stems become bare of leaves in winter and are then harvested to provide the best material for thatching. The fluffy seeds germinate on bare mud in spring.

41. GREATER REED-MACE (*Typha latifolia*). The thick, reddish-brown 'pokers' of this swamp plant develop in late summer and persist through the winter after the leaves have withered. They burst into billows of white, silky seeds during windy weather from March onwards. The seeds are apt to be carried long distances by air and this plant has achieved an almost world-wide distribution in this way, being a universal colonist of mud exposed round ponds and lakes.

42. DEVIL'S-BIT SCABIOUS (*Succisa pratensis*). The heliotrope blossoms of this scabious appear in September amongst rushes in fens and bogs. Their abundant nectar is welcomed by late butterflies, bees and hover-flies when other kinds of flowers are becoming scarce. The reddish-purple pin-head anthers are conspicuous when the flowers first open. In some cases it will be seen that the anthers are white although the flowers look normal in other respects. In such plants the pollen has been replaced by spores of a parasitic smut-fungus.

43. RAYED NODDING BUR-MARIGOLD (*Bidens cernua*, var. *radiata*). Bur-marigolds are annual weeds flowering late in the summer on the muddy fringes of pond and river-flats. As a rule the flower-heads are composed wholly of small greenish-yellow florets, but in the variety illustrated the heads are surrounded by sunflower-like rays. The seeds are crowned with four long, fiercely-barbed spines. These catch on to the fur and plumage of passing animals and birds, causing irritation, so that they have to be removed by scratching and preening in due course; this introduces the seeds to fresh sites.